The Prairie Dog

A Dillon Remarkable Animals Book

The Prairie Dog

By Dorothy Sands Beers

DILLON PRESS, INC.
Minneapolis, Minnesota 55415

Photographic Acknowledgments

A special thank you to W. Perry Conway for supplying most of the photographs in this book. Additional photographs are reproduced through the courtesy of: Dean Biggins/U.S. Fish and Wildlife Service; Colorado Division of Wildlife; William Ervin; Jack Woody/U.S. Fish and Wildlife Service. Cover photograph by W. Perry Conway.

Library of Congress Cataloging-in-Publication Data

Beers, Dorothy Sands.
 The prairie dog / by Dorothy Beers.
  p.   cm. — (A Dillon remarkable animals book)
 Includes bibliographical references.
 Summary: An introduction to the physical characteristics, habits, and natural environment of the member of the squirrel family that lives in underground burrows.
 ISBN 0-87518-444-8 (lib. bdg.) : $12.95
 1. Prairie dogs—United States—Juvenile literature. [1. Prairie dogs.]   I. Title.   II. Series.
 QL737.R68B44   1990
 599.32'32—dc 20   90-3327
                                                              CIP
                                                              AC

© 1990 by Dillon Press, Inc. All rights reserved

Dillon Press, Inc., 242 Portland Avenue South
Minneapolis, Minnesota 55415

Printed in the United States of America
1 2 3 4 5 6 7 8 9 10 99 98 97 96 95 94 93 92 91 90

Contents

Facts about the Prairie Dog 6
1. Prairie Dog Towns 9
2. Life Above and Below Ground 19
3. Home on the Prairie 31
4. A Year on the Prairie 39
5. The War Against Prairie Dogs 47
Glossary 55
Index 58

Facts about the Prairie Dog

Scientific Name: *Cynomys*

Varieties: Black-tailed and white-tailed prairie dogs are the two main species; there are a few other varieties with slightly different coloring

Range: Originally lived on the wide strip of prairie between the Rocky Mountains and the Mississippi River, from Canada in the north to the Gulf of Mexico in the south; at present lives only in spotty areas of the remaining grasslands in this region; the white-tailed prairie dog lives mainly on mountain meadows

Description:
Length—13 to 17 inches (32.5 to 42.5 centimeters)
Height—As tall as four inches (10 centimeters)
Weight—1.5 to 3 pounds (0.7 to 1.4 kilograms)
Life Span—Usually lives four or five years; can live as long as 7 years in the wild
Physical Features—Powerful short legs; long, sharp claws used for digging burrows; excellent eyesight; keen hearing

Distinctive Habits: Lives in a large prairie dog "town"—an amazing network of underground tunnels; sits erect on a mound above ground, watching for predators; gives loud warning alarm calls when danger threatens; also flicks tail when alarmed; sits up to hold plant food in front paws while eating; hugs and kisses other prairie dogs in greeting

Food: Grasses and all parts of plants—the flowers, leaves, stems, and roots; also eats cacti, insects, and grubs

Reproduction: Pairs mate in late winter or early in spring; one litter of two to six pups is born to an adult female in June; this will be her only litter for the year

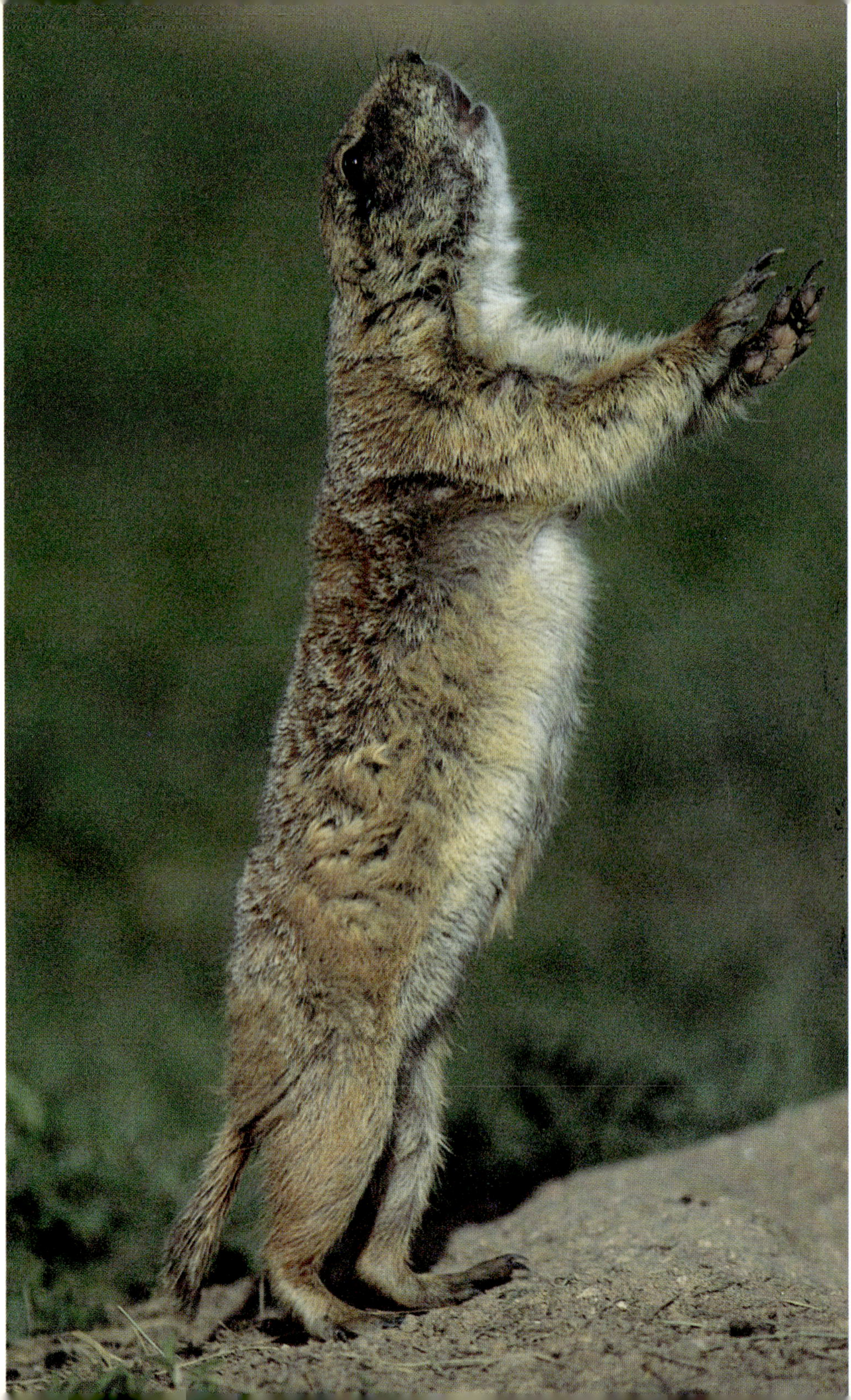

Chapter 1

Prairie Dog Towns

Surrounded by a treeless sea of grass, a plump animal a little larger than a squirrel sits at the entrance to its underground home. Spotting a hawk, it stands up on its short hind legs and sounds a sharp alarm call. Flicking its stubby tail back and forth, it becomes so excited that it falls over backward! Hearing the alarm, more of these creatures begin to bark and squeal, too. They all dive to safety, into their holes in the ground.

These furry animals are called prairie dogs. They are not dogs at all, but members of the squirrel family. Their name came from early French explorers who thought their calls sounded like the barks of *petit chien*, or a little dog.

Prairie dogs live on the prairie grasslands of

A black-tailed prairie dog sounds an alarm call.

The Prairie Dog

North America. These grasslands stretch from southern Canada to northern Mexico, between the Mississippi River and the Rocky Mountains.

A famous student of nature, Ernest Thompson Seton, believed that as many as 5 billion prairie dogs lived on the North American prairie in the 1800s. Today, there are far fewer. When people moved onto the prairie and built farms, ranches, and cities, many prairie dogs were destroyed or forced out.

Prairie dogs dig amazing networks of underground tunnels and rooms, called **burrows**.* These networks of burrows form "towns." A prairie dog town might be the size of a city block or smaller. Or it might be much larger, covering 100 acres (40 hectares).

Prairie dog towns are divided into small communities called **coteries**. Prairie dogs carefully protect and guard their separate communities. One adult male, one or more adult females, and their pups live in an average coterie. But many hundreds of prairie dogs may live in one town.

*Words in **bold type** are explained in the glossary at the end of this book.

This coterie of black-tailed prairie dogs lives in Colorado.

On clear days, some members of a prairie dog town sit by their holes on the lookout for enemies. Meanwhile, other prairie dogs in the town work, eat, or dig more tunnels. But all of these roly-poly animals, no matter what they are doing, have their keen hearing tuned to danger.

Prairie dogs also kiss noses, hug each other,

A mother kisses her pup.

and sunbathe during daylight hours. Members of a coterie work, eat, and relax together. They depend on one another much the way human citizens of a town, village, or city do.

Early Explorers

Two hundred years ago, a huge wilderness known

Prairie Dog Towns

as the Louisiana Territory lay west of the Mississippi River. This land was owned by France. It included millions of acres of grasslands, the area where prairie dogs made their homes.

The United States bought the Louisiana Territory from France in 1804. President Thomas Jefferson sent the famous Lewis and Clark Expedition to find out more about the country's new territory. Captain Merriwether Lewis and George Rogers Clark led the group.

The explorers carefully studied the grasslands and sent reports to the president. Lewis and Clark believed that if settlers moved to these grasslands, they could graze cattle here. The settlers could plow up the land and raise crops, too.

Lewis and Clark reported that the prairie was covered with little animals sitting beside small holes. The explorers had never seen creatures like these before. They tried to capture one to send to President Jefferson. This was a difficult task, because the lively animals dived into

Lewis and Clark noticed that thousands of small holes covered the grasslands.

their burrows whenever people came near.

Unable to capture these creatures above ground, the explorers dug into the earth, hoping to trap one. The burrow was deeper than the explorers expected. When they dug into one hole, the animals escaped down different entrance holes.

Refusing to give up, the explorers carried five

14

heavy barrels of water from a nearby river and flooded a burrow. Finally, they managed to flush out one prairie dog. They put the little animal in a crate and started it off on its long journey to President Jefferson in Washington, the nation's capital.

The trip began in April on a rough wagon ride across the prairie. Next, by boat, the crate floated down the Missouri River and arrived in Saint Louis a month later. From there it traveled down the Mississippi River to New Orleans. Then it sailed by ship from New Orleans to Baltimore on the east coast. Finally, three months after leaving the prairie, the prairie dog reached Washington in another wagon. President Jefferson was delighted with the animal and put it on exhibit in Philadelphia.

Naming the Animal

Scientists carefully studied the small animal. They decided it belonged in a group of animals called *rodentia*. Rodentia is a group or **order** of animals

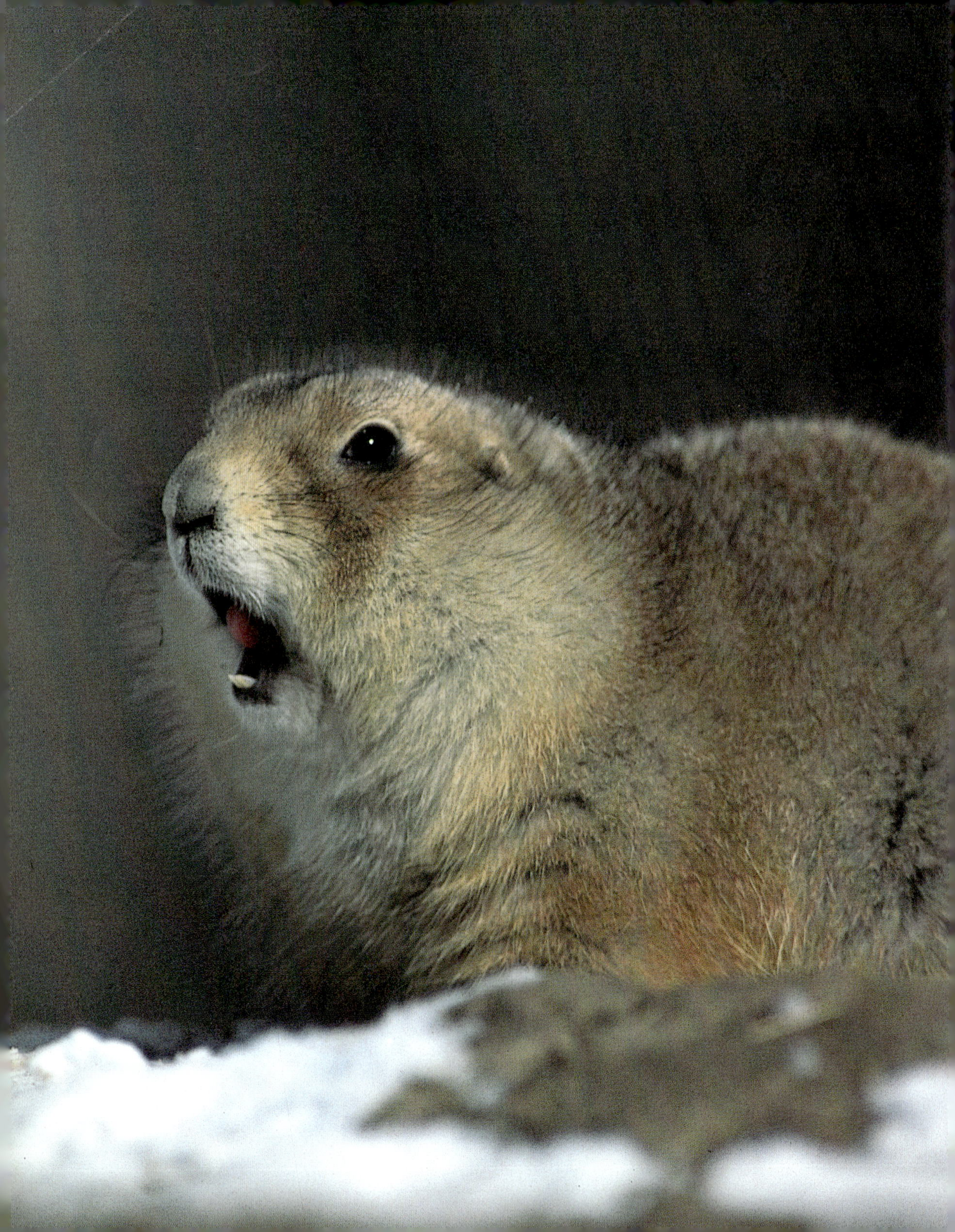

Prairie Dog Towns

that includes **rodents** such as rats, mice, beavers, porcupines, and squirrels. All have four chisel-shaped front teeth called **incisors**. These sharp incisors are used for cutting and gnawing. The words *rodent* and *rodentia* come from the Latin word *rodere*, meaning to gnaw.

Scientists also decided to place the animal in the squirrel, or *sciuridae* family, within the rodentia order. Lastly, the animal was given its own scientific name—*cynomys*—the Greek word for dog. Today, its common name is prairie dog. Like its scientific name, its common name came from the nickname that early French explorers gave the barking animal—little dog.

Like all rodents, the prairie dog has four sharp front teeth.

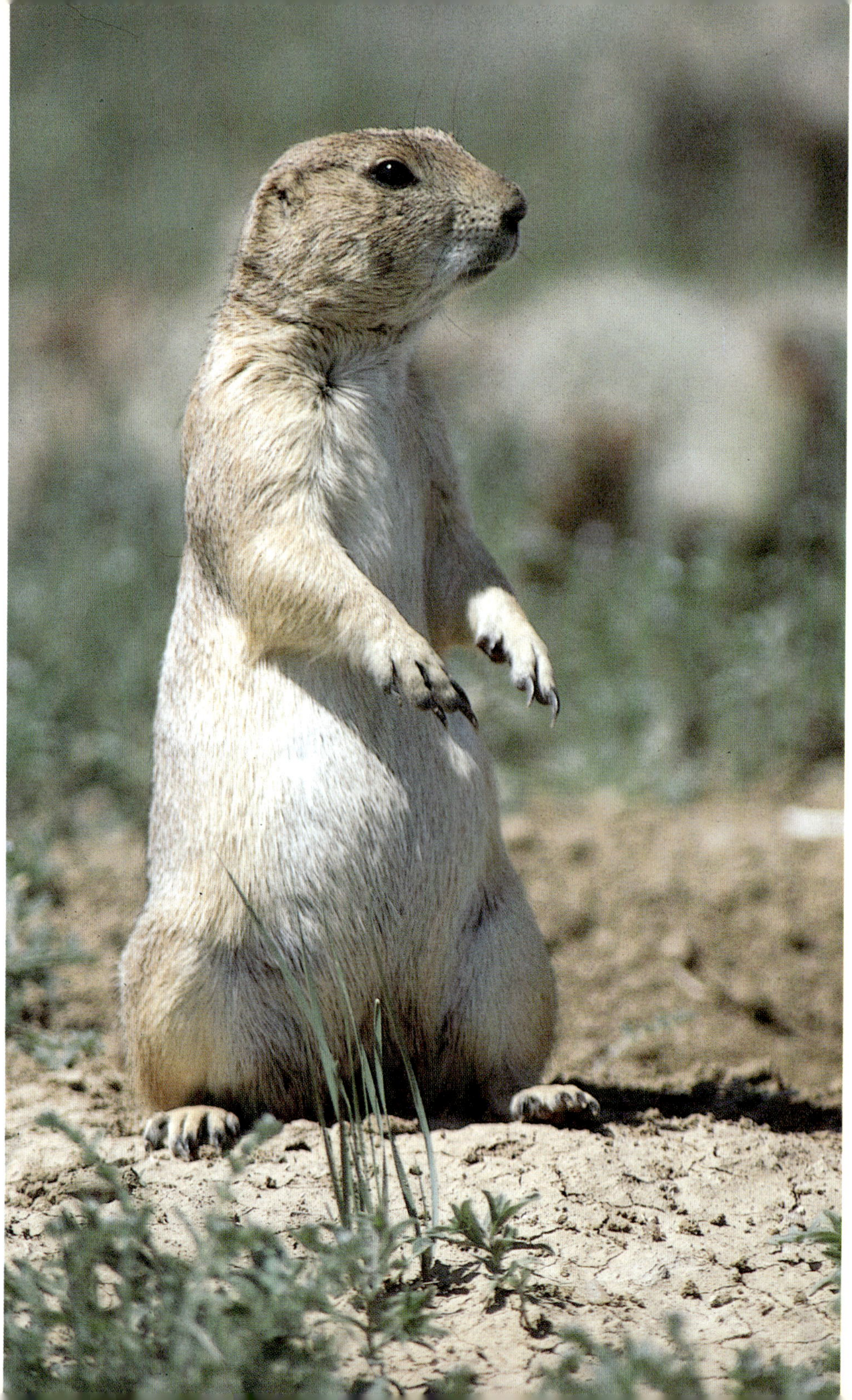

Chapter 2

Life Above and Below Ground

Not all prairie dogs look exactly alike. There are two main **species**, or types, of prairie dogs. These two species have only slight differences. One species has a black tip on its tail, and the other has a white tip.

The most common species, the black-tailed prairie dog, lives on the grasslands of the plains. The white-tailed species lives on high mountain meadows. Less is known about white-tailed prairie dogs. It is difficult to study them since they spend so much time underground in the wintertime.

For a time, scientists thought the red prairie dogs they found in Oklahoma were a separate species. But then they discovered the truth of the matter. These animals were not born with red

This black-tailed prairie dog looks the same as its white-tailed relatives, except that the tip of its tail is darker in color.

The Prairie Dog

fur. They just burrowed in red soil! Likewise, prairie dogs in North Dakota have black-tinted coats from burrowing in the black soil of coal country.

Digging Burrows

With a long, sharp nail on the tip of each of its toes, the prairie dog rips through tough sod and scoops out hard soil. The animal kicks the dirt behind it and up into the air.

A prairie dog tunnel is about 4.5 inches (11.2 centimeters) wide, just large enough for the animals to pass through in single file. It is not possible for them to change directions in this small space. They dig out a side chamber in the tunnel, a short distance from the entrance hole. In this chamber, the prairie dogs stop, turn around, and move back in the opposite direction. They use this room, too, for resting and for listening to noises above ground.

No two prairie dog burrows are exactly alike.

Life Above and Below Ground

Usually, a tunnel goes down into the earth 3 to 15 feet (.9 to 4.6 meters) on a slant. The tunnel then levels out and runs along from 6 to 80 feet (1.8 to 24.4 meters). Gradually, the tunnel rises to another hole leading to the surface in the ground. This hole may serve as either an entrance or an escape hatch.

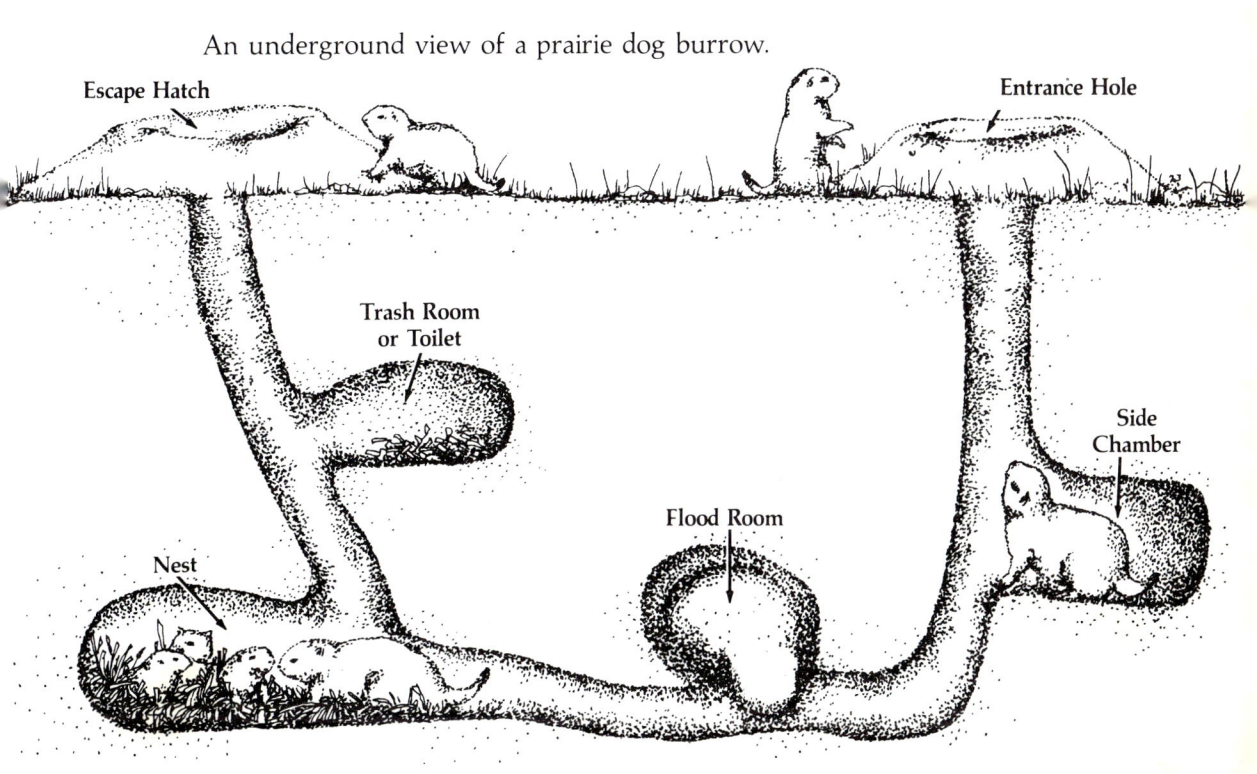

An underground view of a prairie dog burrow.

The Prairie Dog

This deep in the ground, neither freezing temperatures nor the hot blasts of grass fires bother the prairie dog. No matter what the weather is like outside, the temperature deep in the burrow remains comfortable.

Along the tunnel wall, prairie dogs scoop out holes for rooms, just as humans build rooms off of hallways in a house. One chamber in a prairie dog tunnel is about 8 inches wide by 10 inches long (20 by 25 centimeters). It is designed to hold a nest. Other rooms are sometimes used for food storage, for trash (such as old nesting material and loose dirt), or for a place where the burrow members can place their dead.

Some prairie dogs scatter their droppings carelessly anywhere along the tunnels. Others reserve a special toilet room for this purpose.

Most burrows have a flood room dug into the ceiling of a tunnel. As a safety measure, this room serves as an air trap. If a heavy rainfall fills the tunnel, the animals climb up into the flood room.

This room remains dry with plenty of air to breathe until the flood water soaks into the soil.

If prairie dogs need an extra room in their burrow, they simply dig another one out. They might also pack dirt into the entrance of a room that they don't want any longer, to block it off. Prairie dogs often make changes in their homes to suit themselves.

Outside the Burrow

As they dig dirt out of their tunnels, black-tailed prairie dogs take great care to form mounds with the loose dirt. They pack the loose soil into rings that circle the entrance hole to each burrow. Sometimes these rings, or mounds, rise as high as 4 feet (1.2 meters) above ground level.

A burrow mound serves as a **dike**, a bank of earth built to control the flow of water. A mound prevents rainwater from pouring into the tunnels below. If a rainstorm damages a mound, the prairie dogs quickly fix it.

A muddy prairie dog after a rainstorm. Its burrow was flooded because the mound was not built high enough.

During the day, members of a coterie sit outside on their mounds and watch the activities in their town. If weeds block the view in any direction, the prairie dogs snip them off. This way they can observe each other working and playing. But no matter what they are doing—eating, digging, playing, or resting—they always keep a sharp lookout for danger.

Life Above and Below Ground

Alarm Signals

If an alarm call sounds while prairie dogs are away from their mounds, they make a dash for a burrow entrance hole and dive in headfirst. When they reach safety underground, they wait in the side chamber near the surface and listen. Cautiously, they creep up and peer over the mound to make sure the danger has passed.

The prairie dog's loud, barking alarm is only one of its many types of calls. **Naturalists**, people who study plants and animals in nature, have tried to learn the meanings of the various prairie dog calls. Some are friendly chirps to other members of the community. Others tell neighbors from different coteries not to come any closer. Females use a special call when protecting their nests. But the alarm signal is the loudest and longest call of all.

Prairie dogs' tail flicking also sends messages. Prairie dog tails are short, about 3 or 4 inches (7.5 or 10 centimeters) long. They may be short, but they

Two prairie dogs peer over their mound, checking for danger.

move very quickly and attract the attention of other prairie dogs. The more dangerous the situation, the faster the tails flick.

A Prairie Diet

A prairie dog scurries away from its mound on its short legs to feed. It snips off a flower stem or

Life Above and Below Ground

blade of grass. Holding the plant between its front paws, the prairie dog sits up to eat. It eats all the parts of a plant, even the roots. It may eat insects or grubs, too.

The food enters the **cecum**, a storage pouch above the stomach. The cecum is as large and sometimes larger than the stomach itself. It allows the prairie dog to eat more than its stomach alone can hold. This amounts to a great deal of grass. One scientist estimated that 250 prairie dogs eat as much grass as a 1,000-pound (454-kilogram) cow!

Water to Drink?

All animals need water in their bodies. But prairie dogs are rarely seen drinking, not even from puddles after a rainfall. Why don't they drink from puddles? And how can they survive during a drought when it does not rain for months? How do they survive when a grass fire burns all the plants near their town?

Some people have thought that prairie dog

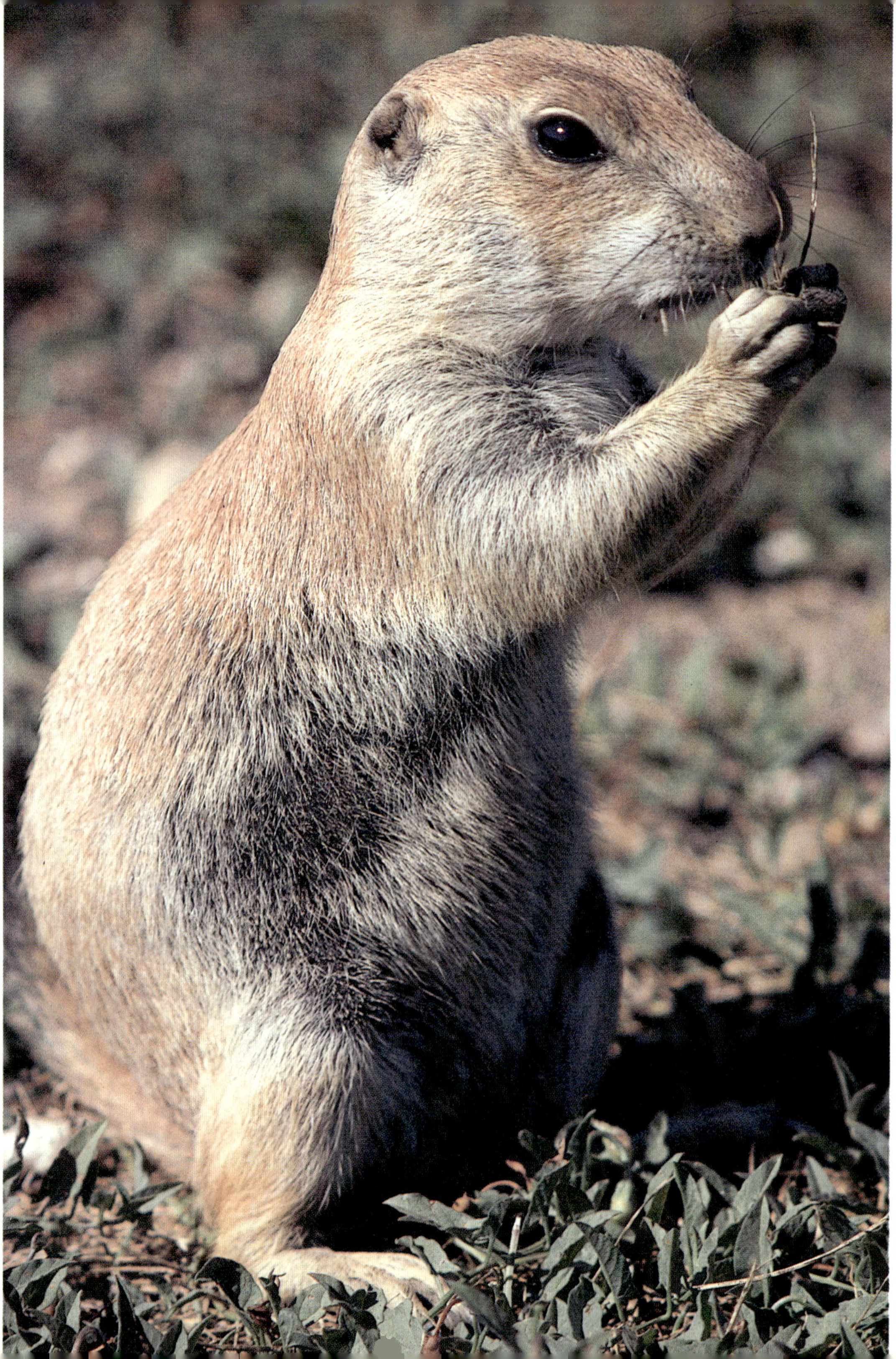

Life Above and Below Ground

towns have community wells dug down to the **water table**. The water table is the level below ground in which the soil is fully soaked with water. Scientists have learned, however, that the water table is far below the lowest part of any prairie dog burrow. Clearly, then, prairie dogs do not have community wells.

Prairie dogs do not need wells. They find enough moisture in juicy plants, insects, and grubs.

A fierce grass fire kills the plants and insects above ground that prairie dogs eat, but fire does not kill a plant's roots. There are plenty of roots on the grasslands for prairie dogs to feed on after a fire. A single rye grass plant can have an underground root system more than 100 miles (161 kilometers) long.

A prairie dog sits up to enjoy its meal of grass.

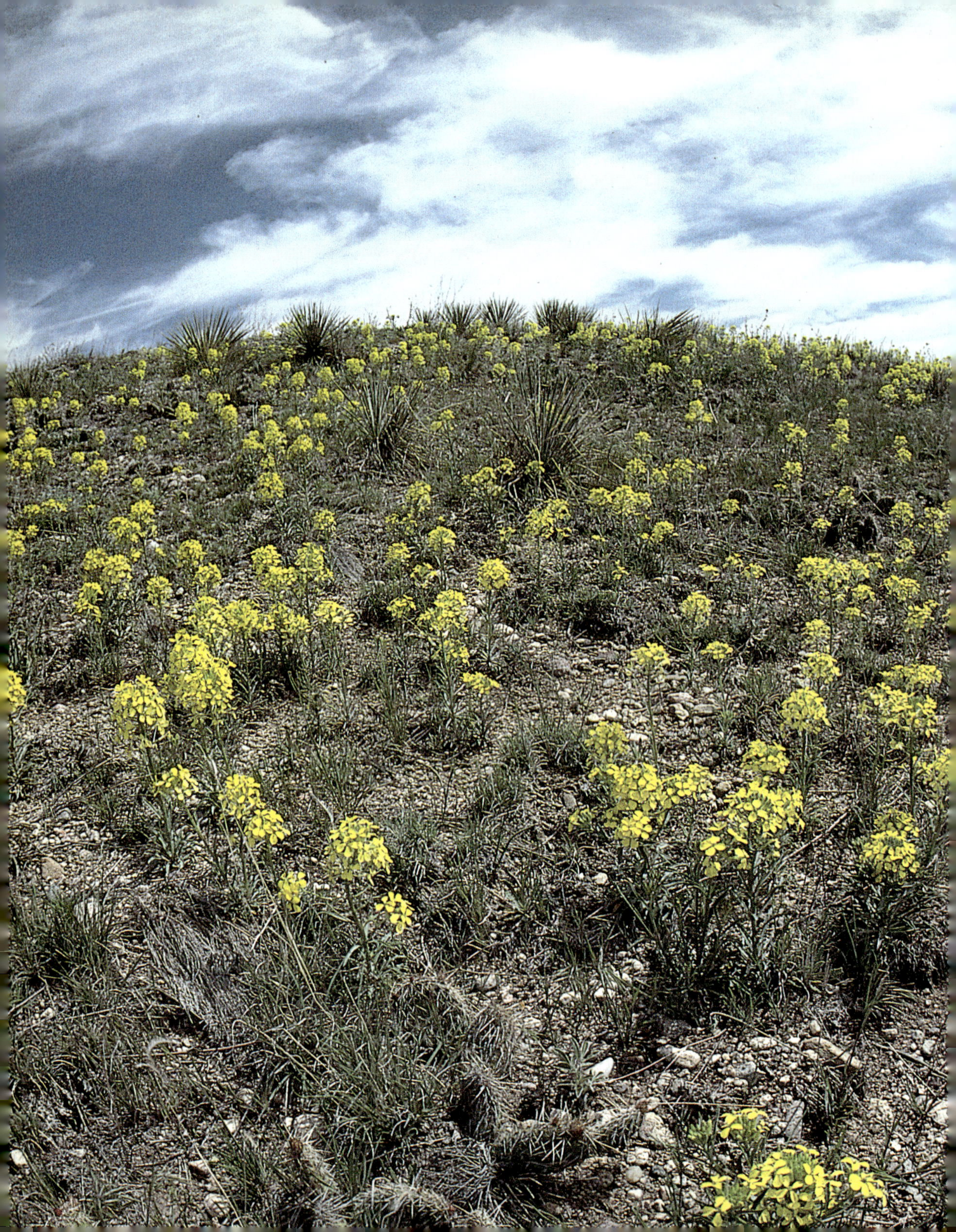

Chapter 3

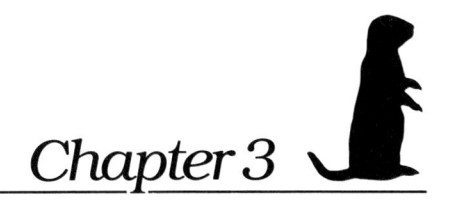

Home on the Prairie

Millions of years ago, the land that later became prairie dog country lay under a sea of water. Over time, the crust of the earth folded, creating a gigantic wrinkle that formed the Rocky Mountains. Hundreds of years passed, and the great sea dried up. A huge flat plain between the Rocky Mountains and the Mississippi River remained. Gradually, a thick carpet of grass grew up and became the prairie.

Today, the prairie stretches about 400 miles (644 kilometers) from east to west, and about 2,000 miles (3,220 kilometers) from north to south. Areas of many states are part of the prairie. These areas include most of Kansas, Oklahoma, Iowa, Nebraska, Illinois, South Dakota, and North Dakota.

Prairie dog country was once covered by a great sea of water.

Parts of other nearby states and southern Canada are also prairie lands.

People who explored the prairie before the time of Lewis and Clark found it dreary. One visitor complained that he could look around in a circle and see nothing but grass. There was not one tree to break the line of the horizon.

Those early human visitors may not have liked the grasslands. But the prairie dog chose the prairie for its **habitat** and has lived on it for thousands of years.

Predators on the Prairie

Prairie dogs share the grasslands with many other creatures. Some of them are **predators** of prairie dogs, which means they hunt them for food.

In spite of these little animals' loud alarm calls, birds such as the red-tailed hawk sometimes catch them for food. The hawk glides in so low to the ground that it is hidden by plant growth. The prairie dogs do not see it until it is too late

Home on the Prairie

to sound their warning calls. Eagles, prairie falcons, and other species of hawks hunt prairie dogs, too.

The small but fierce burrowing owl is another enemy of the prairie dog. Unlike most owls, it is **diurnal**, meaning that it is active during the day rather than at night. Although the burrowing owl

A burrowing owl.

The Prairie Dog

is able to fly, it lives and hunts mostly on the ground. It raids burrows, and feeds on prairie dog pups.

Like the burrowing owl, the rattlesnake also raids prairie dog nests. The rattlesnake is hard for even the watchful prairie dog to see. The markings on its scales blend with prairie grasses to **camouflage** it. A prairie dog might pass right by a rattlesnake and not see it. When the rodent comes near, the snake's jaws snap open. It lunges forward and swallows the rodent headfirst.

Another prairie dog predator is the coyote. Too large to fit into burrows, the coyote tries to capture prairie dogs in surprise attacks. To do so, two coyotes sometimes move onto opposite sides of a town. Alarm calls sound on both sides of the town. A third coyote then crawls on its belly into the unguarded center to hunt.

This trick, however clever, is seldom successful. The prairie dogs' alarm system works too well. If the coyote does capture a prairie dog, it is

This coyote approaches a prairie dog burrow to hunt.

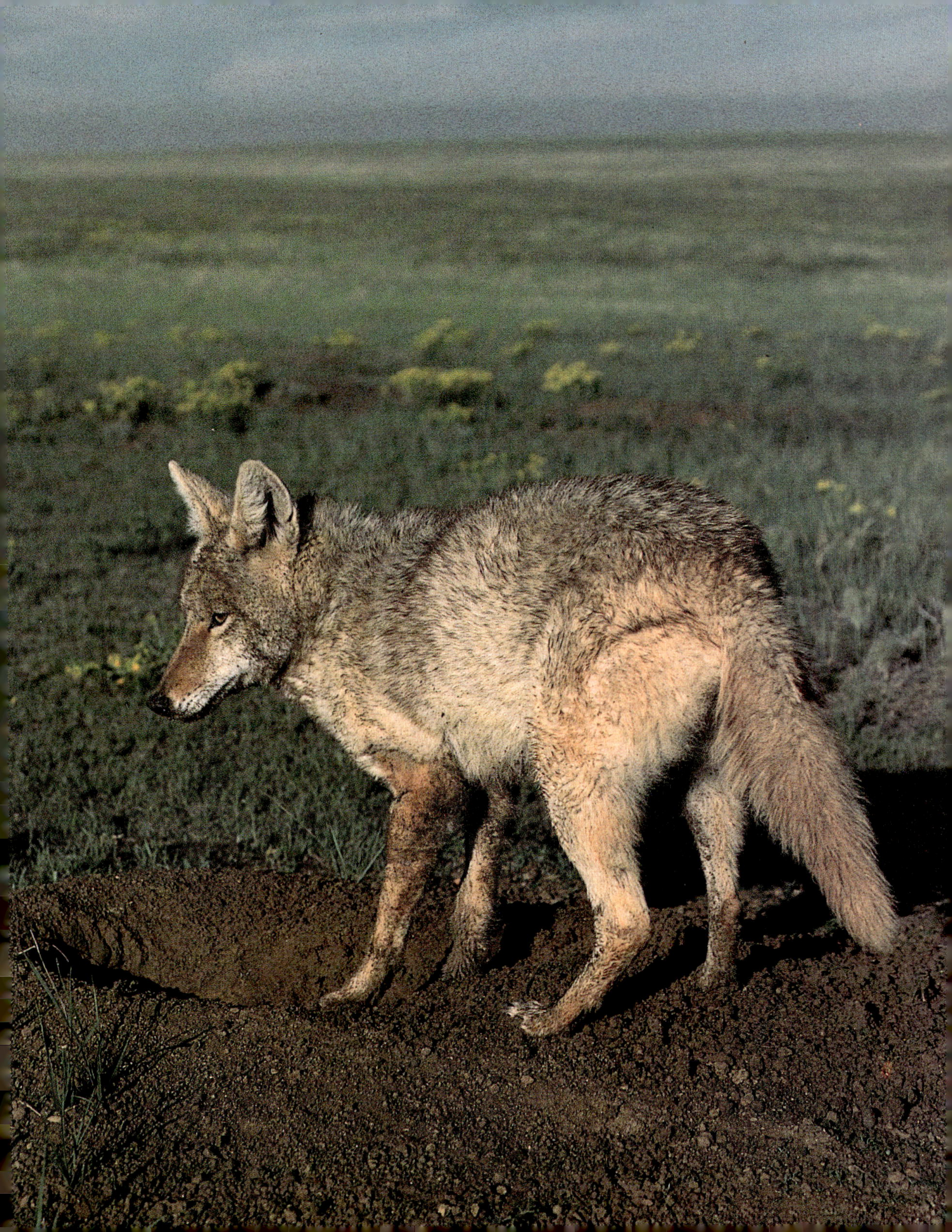

A black-footed ferret.

usually a pup. A pup may not yet have learned what to do at the sound of an alarm call.

The prairie dog's most dangerous natural enemy was the black-footed ferret. For many years, the black-footed ferret ate mainly prairie dogs. Slender, sleek, and swift, the ferret slipped through prairie dog burrows. It chased and hunted

Home on the Prairie

with ease in the darkness of the prairie dogs' underground tunnel system.

Today, however, the black-footed ferret is a problem for few prairie dogs because it is nearly **extinct**. As prairie dogs became scarcer on the plains, the ferrets lost their main source of food and could not survive. The remaining black-footed ferrets live in protected areas.

Although the bison was never a predator of the prairie dog, it caused serious problems for the little animal years ago. Before settlers moved onto the prairie, huge herds of bison thundered over the plains. Their hooves left the soil almost as hard as rock. Digging tunnels and repairing mounds in this hard-packed soil were difficult for the prairie dog.

Over the years, human hunters killed so many bison that they now live mainly in special protected areas. The prairie dog has many predators on the plains. But it is no longer troubled by the black-footed ferret and the bison.

Pups are born and grow up during the warm months on the prairie.

Chapter 4

A Year on the Prairie

Black-tailed prairie dogs spend much of the time during cold winter months underground. Once in a while, the curious animals scratch snow away from their mounds, look around, and move about outside.

As the cold weather nears an end, males wander into different coteries. Meanwhile, females drive away any other prairie dog, male or female, that comes near their burrows.

By February or March, the females' behavior changes. For two or three weeks, they allow males to enter their burrows to mate. Soon it will be time to prepare nests for prairie dog pups.

Spring

In the springtime, prairie dogs scamper about the

The Prairie Dog

coterie, getting to know each other better after the long winter. They carry grasses to their burrows for building nests. Many sit in friendly groups on the mounds, looking like pins set up in a bowling alley.

At this time of year, prairie dogs **molt**. Their fur falls out in patches, making way for a new, lightweight spring coat.

Adult prairie dogs gather grasses to build nests.

A Year on the Prairie

About a month after mating, a female prairie dog gives birth to a **litter** of pups. This litter of two to six pups will be her only litter for the year. The pups are hairless, wrinkled, and helpless. The mother rubs her mouth against them and licks her babies as they nurse.

In two weeks, the pups begin to squirm, squeak, and roll about. They have begun to grow thin coats of fur. After five weeks, the pups' eyes open. They totter around in the dark tunnels near their nest.

While the mother is away eating, predators sometimes enter her burrow in search of newborn pups. A female from a nearby burrow may also raid a nest and destroy an entire litter. While she is at work raiding there, her own nest may be attacked by another female. Mother prairie dogs have been known to eat their own litters. Scientists cannot explain this strange behavior.

Because the pups' lives are so often in danger, only about half of them live to become adults. Males that survive their first year of life can live as long as five years in the wild. Females can live as long as seven years. The pups that do survive their first year can look forward to a happy summer.

The Happy Summer
When the pups are about seven weeks old, they come outside at last. They wobble on their weak legs and blink in the bright sunshine. Their mother still allows them to drink her milk, but only inside the burrow, never outside. As they spend more time outdoors, the pups soon learn to live on plants instead of milk.

On sunny days, the pups chase each other, wrestle, and pounce on insects. Part of their play is learning from adults the important meanings of calls and tail flicking.

During these summer days, adult prairie dogs dig more tunnels and clear out extra rooms. Clouds of dirt fly out of the mounds as they work. While some members dig, others feed or rest. Often pups join their mothers resting on the

When the pups are about seven weeks old, they come outside for the first time and enjoy the summer sunshine.

mounds. They lie together, stretched out on the warm mounds, sunbathing.

Late in the summer, young males leave the burrow where they were born. They move elsewhere, often to an abandoned burrow in the town. Young females stay in the coterie where they were born. They will remain here their entire lives.

The Prairie Dog

The days grow shorter now, and fights begin to break out between coteries as plant food becomes scarcer. The peaceful days of summer have come to an end.

Autumn

By September, the pups are almost full grown. The days are shorter, and much colder. To prepare for winter, prairie dogs eat a great deal of food during the autumn months. They put on a thick layer of fat. In the winter months to come, they will lose this weight. There will be little or no plant food left for them to eat.

Again, the prairie dogs molt. They grow thicker, warmer coats. During the winter, the harsh weather will force them to spend most of the time underground. They clean their burrows before their long underground stay, scattering their waste outside.

The prairie grasses are now brown and dry. Cold winds and snow blow over the plains. Snug inside their protected tunnels, the prairie dogs are ready for the harsh winter months ahead.

Life on Mountain Meadows

The year is different for white-tailed prairie dogs. They live on meadows, high in the mountains. Warm spring weather may not arrive until July in this harsh climate. It may snow even during the summer months. Winter comes earlier here than it does on the plains, so white-tailed prairie dogs have more work to do in fewer warm days than their black-tailed relatives.

The short, warm season is spent digging burrows, raising the young, and eating. The white-tailed rodents must eat as much as they can to store fat for the long winter.

Life has always been hard for white-tailed prairie dogs. Mountain weather is harsh, and the summers are short. But their hard work in the summertime pays off. When autumn arrives, they are well prepared for the long winter months underground.

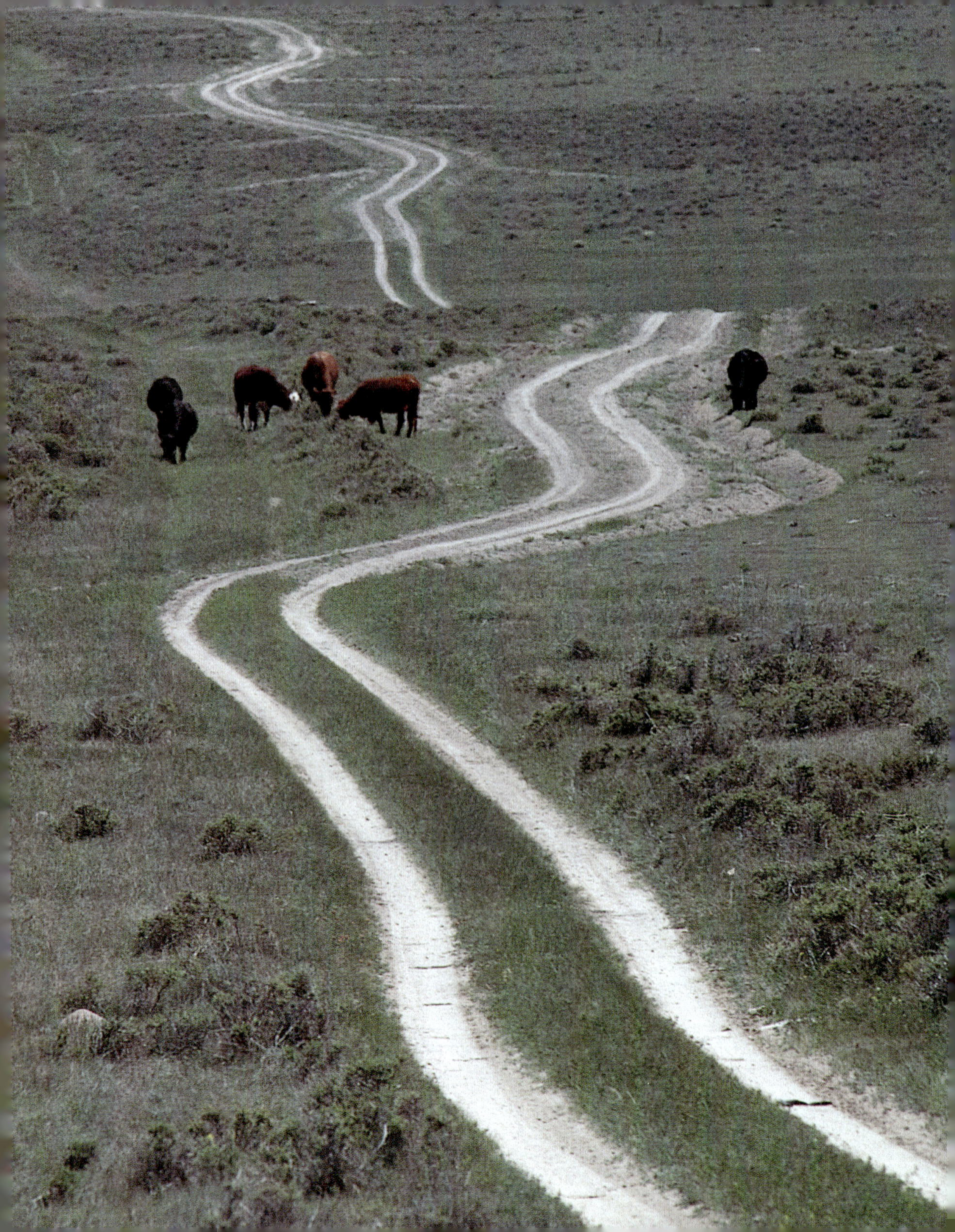

Chapter 5

The War Against Prairie Dogs

As soon as pioneers moved onto the prairie in the 1800s, many of them disliked prairie dogs. The little animals began to compete with cattle for grass. They also began to eat the settlers' row crops, such as cotton and wheat. Some horses and cattle broke legs in prairie dog holes, too. As time passed, ranchers and farmers feared that prairie dogs would cause even more problems.

One worry was that prairie dogs, like other rodents, sometimes carried the **bubonic plague**. This disease was passed on by fleas that had caught it from infected rats. Bubonic plague was often a deadly disease. The early settlers knew they could catch it from a flea bite, if the flea had first bitten an infected prairie dog.

Early ranchers and farmers feared that their cattle would break legs in prairie dog holes.

The Prairie Dog

Settlers found it hard to get rid of prairie dogs. One shot of a gun would send a whole town diving underground to safety.

By 1900, landowners began to ask for help from the government. The government agreed the problem was serious. In the 1920s, local and state governments began to help farmers and ranchers destroy prairie dogs. The government of the United States joined in the effort. Poison gas was pumped into burrows. Government workers scattered poisoned grain and corn around mounds and in burrows. Planes dropped poisoned grain onto acres of prairie grasslands. Millions of prairie dogs died. In Kansas alone, over a 50-year period, prairie dogs on 2.5 million acres (1 million hectares) were destroyed.

The Value of Prairie Dogs

It was not until the 1950s that the poisoning program slowed down. Concerned citizens began to see its serious results. At this rate, they realized,

The War Against Prairie Dogs

prairie dogs might become extinct. Other wild animals and farm animals, too, were dying from the poison.

People worried about the effects the poison might have on their children and pets. They also wondered if the poison would seep into rivers and reservoirs that supplied their cities with water.

Concerned groups, such as the National Audubon Society, tried to stop the poisoning. They understood the problems that prairie dogs caused. But they also pointed out the value of the animals. These rodents dug up hard-packed soil, they said. This **aerated** the soil, making it loose and supplying it with air. Plants could grow roots more easily in the lighter soil. Also, rainwater collected in prairie dog burrows. This allowed moisture to sink more deeply into the earth and helped plants to grow.

The concerned groups pointed out that prairie dogs' burrowing brought minerals and fertile bottom soil to the surface. Stronger, healthier plants grew in this rich soil. And as for spreading the

The Prairie Dog

bubonic plague, they said, few, if any, cases among humans had ever been traced directly to prairie dogs.

Rescue Programs

Today, some prairie dogs are still being poisoned, but only in small areas. The most serious threat to prairie dogs now comes from the growth of towns and cities. New roads, buildings, and parking lots mean that prairie dog towns have been flattened and covered with pavement.

Groups such as Prairie Dog Rescue and the Humane Society have helped save many prairie dogs. When these groups learn of a plan to build over a prairie dog town, they capture as many of the little animals as possible and move them to a safe new location.

Rescuers have found they cannot simply drop prairie dogs on new land and expect them to start a town. In a state of shock, the animals act dazed and do not survive. They do best if left near aban-

Prairie dog towns are often flattened by machines, to build new roads and parking lots.

doned burrows. Here, they move into ready-made tunnels and soon feel right at home.

The Future of the Prairie Dog

Today, airplane passengers arriving in Denver and other western airports see prairie dogs sitting on mounds beside airport runways. Motorists often

A curious prairie dog peeks out of its burrow at the scientist's camera.

The War Against Prairie Dogs

see prairie dogs beside superhighways. People all over the prairie can watch these roly-poly, barking burrowers at work and at play in park exhibits and zoos.

Scientists watch prairie dogs closely, too. There is still much to learn about these amazing animals and their remarkable towns. With protection, prairie dogs will continue to live, burrow, and bark on western grasslands for many years to come.

Glossary

aerate (AIR-ate)—to supply with air

bubonic plague (byoo-BAHN-ihk playg)—a serious and sometimes deadly disease spread by fleas and ticks

burrow—a tunnel or hole dug in the ground by an animal, where the animal lives or hides

cecum (SEE-kum)—a large storage section above the stomach

camouflage (CAM-uh-flahj)—the coloring or patterns of an animal's fur or skin, which helps it hide from predators or enemies

coterie (KOT-uh-ree)—a small community in a prairie dog town

dike—a wall built to hold back water and to prevent flooding

diurnal (die-URN-ehl)—active mainly during daylight hours

extinct (ehk-STINGKT)—no longer living anywhere on earth; many plant and animal species have become extinct

habitat (HAB-ih-tat)—the area where a plant or animal naturally lives

incisors (in-SIE-zuhrz)—front teeth that are large and sharp, used for cutting or gnawing

litter—all of the animal babies born at one time to the same mother

molt—to shed fur or skin which is replaced with a new coat or skin

naturalist—a person who studies nature

order—a group of related people, animals, or things; animals with four sharp front teeth belong to the rodent order

predator (PREHD-uh-tuhr)—an animal that hunts other animals for food

rodent (ROH-duhnt)—one of a large family of animals with four sharp front teeth used for cutting or gnawing

species (SPEE-sheez)—distinct kinds of animals or plants that have common characteristics and a common name

water table—the level below ground in which the soil is fully soaked with water

Index

adaptation, 50-52
aeration, 49
alarm call, 25, 34
appearance, 9, 19, 20
bark, 19, 25
behavior, 11-12, 24, 39
black-footed ferret, 36-37
bubonic plague, 47, 50
burrows, 10, 22-23, 44, 49
camouflage, 34
cecum, 27
Clark, George Rogers, 13, 14-15
claws, 20
coteries, 10
dikes, 23
extinction, 37, 49
food, 26-27, 28
habitat, 9-10, 13, 19, 32, 45
Humane Society, 50
Jefferson, President Thomas, 13
Lewis, Merriwether, 13, 14-15
life span, 42
Louisiana Territory, 13

mating, 39, 41
molting, 40, 44
naturalists, 25
National Audubon Society, 49
nests, 22, 40
nickname, 9, 17
poisons, 48, 49, 50
population, 10
prairie dog: black-tailed, 19, 39; white-tailed, 19, 45
prairies, 31-32
Prairie Dog Rescue, 50
prairie dog towns, 10
predators, 32-34
pups, 36, 41, 42, 43, 44
range, 10, 31
relatives, 15, 17
Seton, Ernest Thompson, 10
settlers, 47, 48
tails, 25-26
teeth, 17
tunnels, 20-21

About the Author

Dorothy Sands Beers often watches the activities in a prairie dog town within the city limits of Boulder, Colorado, where she lives. She is a member of the Colorado Mountain Club, and hikes every week on the plains and in the mountains. Ms. Beers has been published in a variety of children's magazines. *The Prairie Dog* is her second book for children. She lives in Boulder with her husband and is the mother of two grown children.